HOW YOU TALK

HOW YOU TALK

By PAUL SHOWERS

Illustrated by
ROBERT GALSTER

THOMAS Y. CROWELL COMPANY
NEW YORK

LET'S-READ-AND-FIND-OUT SCIENCE BOOKS

Editors: *DR. ROMA GANS*, Professor Emeritus of Childhood Education, Teachers College, Columbia University

DR. FRANKLYN M. BRANLEY, Chairman and Astronomer of The American Museum–Hayden Planetarium

Air Is All Around You

Animals in Winter

A Baby Starts to Grow

Bees and Beelines

Before You Were a Baby

The Big Dipper

Big Tracks, Little Tracks

Birds at Night

Birds Eat and Eat and Eat

The Blue Whale

The Bottom of the Sea

The Clean Brook

Down Come the Leaves

A Drop of Blood

Ducks Don't Get Wet

The Emperor Penguins

Find Out by Touching

Fireflies in the Night

Flash, Crash, Rumble, and Roll

Floating and Sinking

Follow Your Nose

Glaciers

Gravity Is a Mystery

Hear Your Heart

High Sounds, Low Sounds

How a Seed Grows

How Many Teeth?

How You Talk

Hummingbirds in the Garden

Icebergs

In the Night

It's Nesting Time

Ladybug, Ladybug, Fly Away Home

The Listening Walk

*Look at Your Eyes**

A Map Is a Picture

The Moon Seems to Change

My Five Senses

My Hands

My Visit to the Dinosaurs

North, South, East, and West

Rain and Hail

Rockets and Satellites

Salt

Sandpipers

Seeds by Wind and Water

Shrimps

The Skeleton Inside You

Snow Is Falling

Spider Silk

Starfish

*Straight Hair, Curly Hair**

The Sun: Our Nearest Star

The Sunlit Sea

A Tree Is a Plant

Upstairs and Downstairs

Watch Honeybees with Me

What Happens to a Hamburger

What I Like About Toads

What Makes a Shadow?

What Makes Day and Night

*What the Moon Is Like**

Where Does Your Garden Grow?

Where the Brook Begins

Why Frogs Are Wet

The Wonder of Stones

*Your Skin and Mine**

*AVAILABLE IN SPANISH

4   5   6   7   8   9   10

ISBN 0-690-42135-4   0-690-42136-2 (LB)

HOW YOU TALK

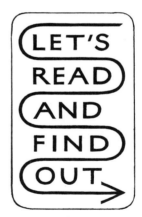

LET'S
READ
AND
FIND
OUT

My baby sister is seven months old.
Her name is Kate, and she is learning to talk.
No one can understand what she says.
But that does not stop her. She talks all the time.

She says, "Ga ga ga ga ga."

She says, "Na na na na na."

NA NA NA NA NA

NA NA

Sometimes she blows air through her lips,
"Pbpbpbpbpbpb,"
or she makes a buzzing sound,
"Dzzzzzzzzzzzz."

"She's doing all right," my father says.
"Don't stop her. Kate is working hard.
"She is learning to make the sounds we use when we
talk."

Sue, who lives across the street, has a little brother.
   He is three years old.
His name is Rufus and he is learning to talk, too.
Rufus talks much better than Kate.
You can understand him.
He can say almost anything, but he doesn't always say
   it right.

He can't quite say his name.
He says, "My name is Wufus."

Rufus has a rabbit. His name is Solomon.

Rufus can say *Solomon* pretty well, but he can't say
  rabbit.
He calls Solomon a "wabbit."

"Never mind," Father says. "Give Rufus time to learn.
"He doesn't know all the ways to use his tongue.
"He still makes too many sounds with his lips."

Sue and I wanted to find out how we make sounds
  when we talk.
You can find out, too.

First, stand up and put your hands on your chest.
Feel your ribs with your fingers.
Inside your ribs are your lungs.
Close your mouth and take a deep breath.
As you breathe in, your chest swells out.

Air goes in your nose, down through your throat, and
  into your lungs.
Breathe in as much as you can.
Now say *Ahhhhhhhh* and let the air out s-l-o-w-l-y.
Keep on saying *Ahhhhh* as long as you can.
You can say it as long as some air is in your lungs.
When you run out of air, you run out of *Ahhhhhhhh*.
You have to use your lungs when you talk.

AHHHHH--H-H

Ahhh-hh--h-h

AH

Take another deep breath.

Tip your head back and feel your throat with your fingertips.

Breathe out again and say *Ahhhhhhh.*

Can you feel the place in your throat where the sound is made?

AHHHH - - H - H - HHHH

Ask your father to say *Ahhhh*. Feel his throat as he
says it.

The place where the sound is made is called the larynx.

Sometimes your larynx is called your voice box.
But it isn't really a box.
It is a place in your throat where air goes through a
narrow opening.
Air goes down through your larynx when you breathe
in.
It goes up through your larynx when you breathe out.
Either way, you can breathe without making a sound.

But when you want to make a sound,
when you want to talk or sing,
then you use your larynx.

Here is how your larynx works. Get a balloon and
  pretend the balloon is your lungs.
Pretend the neck of the balloon is your throat.
Blow up the balloon.

Hold the neck of the balloon shut with both hands.

Stretch the opening of the balloon so that it makes a
narrow slit.

As the air comes through the slit, it makes a squealing
sound.

If the slit is narrow the squeal is high.

As the slit gets wider the squeal goes lower.

18

Your larynx works something
like the slit in the balloon.
But it works much better.

You use it to make ALL KINDS OF SOUNDS.

When Kate makes her funny sounds, she is learning
  to use her larynx.
She is learning to make
  high sounds

low sounds

loud sounds

soft sounds.

23

Hold a mirror up to your mouth.
Curl back your lips and show your teeth.

Open your mouth
and stick out your tongue.

Tap your upper teeth
with the tip of your tongue.

Close your mouth and hum.

25

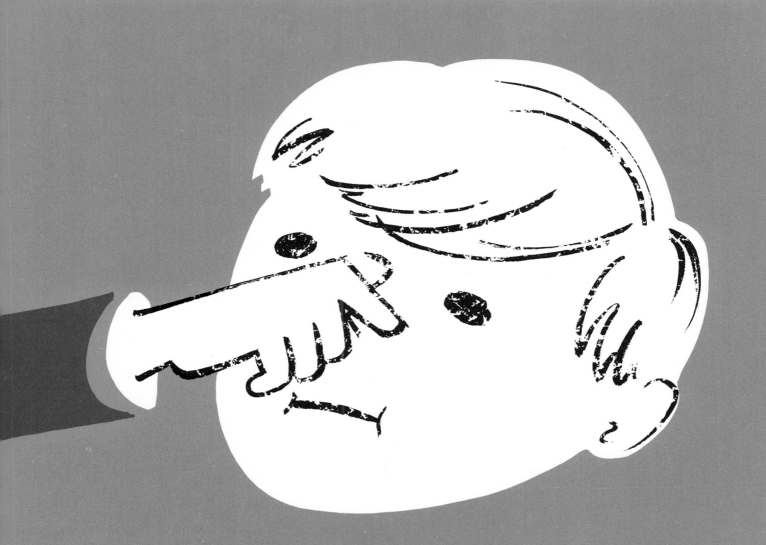

Keep on humming and pinch the end of your nose shut
with your fingers.

Let go. Now pinch it shut again.

Say, "My, my, my" and "No, no, no" and "Ding, ding,
ding."

You use your nose when you hum.

You use it when you make the sounds for *m* and *n* and
ng.

Watch your mouth in the mirror and make these
sounds:

Ma-ah-ah-ah

Me-ee-ee-ee

Moo-oo-oo-oo.

You change the sound when you change the shape of
  your mouth.
When you talk you use
  your lungs
     your larynx
       your mouth
         your nose
           your lips
             your tongue
               your teeth.

MA-AH-AH-AH-AH

ME-EE-EE-EE

MOO-OO-OO-OO

How do you use your lips?

Look in the mirror and say,

　"Beans and bananas, butterflies and bread."

Say it again slowly and watch your lips.

Can you say these words without using your lips?

Try it.

Open your mouth wide. Watch your lips in the mirror.

　Keep them wide apart.

Don't let your lips touch.

Say, "Beans and bananas."

Say, "Butterflies and bread."

Can you do it?

Rufus uses his lips sometimes when he should use his tongue.

You have to use your tongue when you say,
   "Rabbits and ribbons, rockets and rope."
You use your tongue for other sounds.

Try this.

Open your mouth and hold down your tongue with the
spoon.

Say, "Rabbits and ribbons, rockets and rope."

Say, "Lemons and lollipops, lizards and lace."

You use your teeth when you talk.

Open your mouth. Look in the mirror and say,
"Thick, thin, thumbs, and Thursday."

Watch how your tongue touches your teeth. Say,
"This, that, these, and they."

People use many kinds of sounds when they talk.
It takes a long time to learn how to make these sounds.
Kate is just beginning to learn how.
She can say *ga ga ga* but she can't say *garage*.
Rufus is still learning to talk.
He can say, "I am a big boy." But he still calls Solomon
a "wabbit."

Sue and I like to hear Rufus talk.
He says funny things.
But we don't make fun of him.
We wouldn't want to hurt his feelings.

My father says: "Never talk baby talk to a baby.
He is doing the best he can.
He is not trying to be funny. He is just trying to talk."
When Sue and I play with Rufus, we pay no attention
   to his mistakes.
We help Rufus pick leaves to feed to Solomon.
But we always call Solomon a *rabbit*.
We never say "*wabbit*" the way Rufus does.
Some day, Father says, Rufus will say "*rabbit*," too.

34402

J
612 S
SHOWERS
  HOW YOU TALK

s 6/03 Lu 7/01 3 circ 3 lib

7